Let's Talk

Let's Talk

JESSIE YENDLE

■ **SCHOLASTIC**

Published in the UK by Scholastic, 2023
1 London Bridge, London, SE1 9BG
Scholastic Ireland, 89E Lagan Road, Dublin Industrial Estate,
Glasnevin, Dublin, D11 HP5F

SCHOLASTIC and associated logos are trademarks and/or
registered trademarks of Scholastic Inc.

Text © Jessie Yendle, 2023
All photographs © Jessie Yendle, 2023, except
pages 62–63 © The Wedding Guys 2023
Illustrations © Shutterstock, 2023
Quotations on pages 25, 34, 80, 89, 107 and 121 © Matthew Taylor Wilson, 2023

The right of Jessie Yendle to be identified as the author of this work has been asserted
by her under the Copyright, Designs and Patents Act 1988.

ISBN 978 07023 2923 4

A CIP catalogue record for this book is available from the British Library.

Any website addresses listed in the book are correct at the time of going to print.
However, please be aware that online content is subject to change and websites can
contain or offer content that is unsuitable for children.

Printed and bound in Italy.
Paper made from wood grown in sustainable forests and other controlled sources.

1 3 5 7 9 10 8 6 4 2

www.scholastic.co.uk

I WANNA DEDICATE THIS BOOK TO LITTLE JESSIE, SHE WAS A LITTLE DELICATE FLOWER BUD WHO NEVER THOUGHT SHE WAS CAPABLE OF BLOSSOMING.

EVERYONE'S GROWTH IS DIFFERENT. FOREVER BE YOUR TRUE, AUTHENTIC, ORIGINAL SELF AND BLOOM FREELY.

CONTENTS

CONTENTS

CONTENTS

WELCOME HOME!

Let this book be your safe place. Read it in the bath, in your bed, on the beach, wherever you want. You can even draw in it, tear it, whatever you like – just allow this book to be your best friend in your pocket.

Throughout my life I wish I had an older best friend or big sis to guide me through and help me to deal with my thoughts and emotions. Someone to show me how to take care of my mind and most importantly how to **LOVE MYSELF**, even on those days when the rain is pouring down a little harder. I hope I can be your best friend or big sis on this journey.

Now I'm a grown woman, I want to share my life experiences, lessons, challenges and journey in which I conquered so many fears.

So allow me to welcome you home, this is YOUR safe place. Let's start our journey together.

ME, MYSELF AND I

Allow me to introduce myself fully, so you can know me on a first name basis before diving into the thick of it.

My official legal name is Jessica but the only time I ever hear that is when I'm in deep trouble, so I go by the name Jessie. I guess many people know me as "That Girl Off TikTok With a Stammer", who is constantly going through the drive-through or handing out flowers to strangers, working on her self-love. All my life I've struggled with anxiety, panic attacks, fitting in, wanting to be liked, and pushing my own feelings aside to make other people happy. Over the years, I have begun to realize that I've got a big heart but boundaries are key.

I won't lie to you, in the words of Ronan Keating: life is a rollercoaster, and I feel like I've been sat on that rollercoaster with my hands in the air enjoying the ride, but terrified at the same time.

Every great adventure happens when you decide to not give up.

I had always seen my stammer as a curse, but as cringe as it sounds, it's now my superpower and I wouldn't change it for the biggest box of caramel chocolates in the world (even if you tried tempting me with a cheeky white mocha and hazelnut frappé, which is my absolute favourite right now).

Just like the start of an *X Factor* audition, here's my story. It's March 1993 and I was birthed into this beautiful, wonderful world. As I turned from a baby into a little girl, I started to struggle with my speech development.

When I was four years old, I was still unable to get my words out, so I started tapping my chest to indicate the word "me". As the years went on, it became obvious that I was still struggling to speak and I began to notice that I was not like my other friends at school. I felt different, like a spare sock that had been left behind.

One day I remember being so frustrated about trying to answer a question from my teacher and that's when a man took me out of class. I thought I was in trouble, sitting in the headteacher's office, but little did I know it was the day that would change my entire life. I was told that I had a stammer.

I didn't understand what that was at first, and I was scared and confused. It's a lot to take in as a young child but I started speech therapy and thought I would be cured from this struggle. Unfortunately, speech therapy wasn't right for me. I tried many different speech programmes in my teens but the one thing which ended up really working for me was building my self-confidence, taking on the mindset of self-belief, and learning that how you talk to yourself is **POWERFUL**. People call it manifesting, or you might have heard about something called "lucky girl syndrome" (when if you believe you're lucky, good things will come to you) but this book is where I'm gonna share my secrets of living your best life and

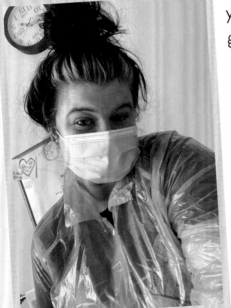

how to be the best version of yourself, no matter what you're going through.

So how did I grow my family of millions online? Well, in October 2021 I had just finished my 24-hour shift as a support worker and it was roughly 10.30am in the morning. I was feeling exhausted and whilst on my journey home I drove past a coffee shop. It was in that moment that I decided today was gonna be the day that I faced my fear of talking to strangers by ordering a coffee. I sat in the car park for a while, hyping myself up. I decided to film myself on my phone making the order, as I never answered calls, ordered coffee or ordered my food at a restaurant on my own, so this was a **BIGGIE**.

I placed my order, got my coffee and drove home. I immediately sent the video to my family and friends. I felt incredible, like I had just won the lottery. Riding off the back of this feeling, I decided to post my video onto social media. As I put my phone down, I decided not to look at any of the comments, as after living my life up till then feeling misunderstood, I remember worrying, "Is the world ready to see something like this on social media?"

Little did I know, my video went viral with millions of people showing me unmatched love and support, and so my journey was born. That day a video wasn't just uploaded – a movement was started.

I started to challenge my speech daily in order to grow my confidence because I knew nothing could grow inside my comfort zone and you've gotta make the uncomfortable finally feel comfortable. I walked up to strangers with a stomach full of nerves and my heart racing, handing them flowers whilst also telling them about my stammer. My voice shook, but every single time these people respected my determination.

This brings me to one of my favourite sayings which is "You can't influence the world by being like it." I truly believe my stammer is now a gift, it's made me the person I am today and as each day goes on it gives me the strength to never give up.

My stammer had made me a prisoner inside my own body and mind. As a little girl I had never wanted to get married or become a mother due to my speech, but today I'm writing this book as a wife, with dreams of becoming a mum.

So much is taken for granted. For people who don't have speech impediments, even the power of having a **VOICE** can be taken for granted.

On my journey I've learned that true happiness comes from within, not by impressing society with materialistic objects. So let's go hand in hand on this journey. Now you know my story and how I got here, I hope you're ready to change your life, mindset and power.

Let's talk!

JESSIE X

30TH B'DAY

LITTLE JESSIE'S CAREER PATH

I think my nose would grow like Pinocchio's if I told you that Little Jessie wanted to have only one job, because growing up I never knew what I wanted to be as an adult. There's just so much pressure on kids to know what they want to do at such a young age. If anyone asked I would say a nurse, a vet or a teacher but honestly I also just loved going wild with a pot of paint.

In high school I had do a week of work experience – can you imagine my face when I was told that I was being sent to a loud, bustling and chatty hairdressers?! I was placed on the front desk and I will forever remember being petrified of the phone. Every time it rang I wanted to run all the way home. Even in the early noughties there was no extra support for me and my stammer, I just had to get through it. But luckily this led me on a path where I found happiness from doing what I enjoyed.

Being a child who couldn't verbally communicate well, I would often express myself through painting, the way I dressed, and makeup. These expressions included using blue food dye in my hair and the many weird but wonderful hairstyles which ruined every annual school photograph.

Art became my voice and the moment I picked up a camera for the first time, I felt like I knew that that was my calling in life. I went on to study Photography in my A Levels along with Art and Textiles, then I studied Fashion and Advertising Photography at university. I was winging it like an eyeliner wing being drawn on in a rush. I had no idea what my future looked like but I was **HAPPY** and fulfilled.

Little Jessie had no set plan and no firm career path, she went with what made her happy, what she enjoyed daily and what brought her purpose. Never feel like you're failing, because the universe probably has a plan and a path for you. Invest your energy into what brings you **PURE HAPPINESS!**

27

my MORNING ROUTINE!

Let's be real – a routine is impossible to stick to, but I'm gonna share my morning routine which not only helps my anxiety but leads me to have a more productive day.

STEP 1

First thing I do is my cold water morning face bath (for full instructions on this, see pages 38–39). Once complete you're gonna feel like a brand new freshly born baby. Also did I mention that this works wonders for your skin? Trust me on this.

STEP 2

Get a large water bottle – I don't care if it's pink, blue, multicoloured or clear, just grab it and fill it with ice-cold tap water. Carry this round with you so you can always be hydrated.

STEP 3

I then go for a healthy breakfast. The word HEALTHY puts me off any kind of food so I tend to have porridge spruced up with a dash of chocolate and hazelnut spread plus bananas or strawberries. This fills me up until lunch and is super quick and easy to make.

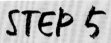

STEP 4

I then take a quick shower using all my feel-good products and, after the singing performance of a lifetime has taken place, I dry off and move on to my skincare.

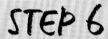

STEP 5

Looking after the skin you're in is highly important and part of my daily routine. We will go into this in more detail later on (see pages 122–125) but I like to use a face mask, serums, lotions and potions, and I feel incredible straight away.

STEP 6

After my feel good session I ALWAYS get dressed. I can't stress how important this is. It's so easy to sit around in your PJs but, fact of the matter is, it's not doing any favours for your mental health or productivity. You will feel 1,000% better by popping on some clothes and feeling fresh. Just please don't wear jeans if you're home all day, as that's a crime!

STEP 7

After my feel good routine, I then crack on with my to-do list which I always make the night before. Time is precious and we gotta use it wisely.

HOW THE TUTTI FRUTTI DID I GET HERE?

Let's bring it back like a throwback anthem and put our hands in the air because I ask myself daily, "How am I, Jessie Yendle writing a book, and am an author when I failed my English GCSEs 3 or 4 times?"

The secret sauce is **SELF-BELIEF**. The fear of failure and looking silly is holding you back.

We are told we **NEED** to be academic in school to be successful, but we are never told how important it is to have the tools and mindset of someone positive and confident, and how vital showing self-love can be.

Basically I want this to be your daily reminder that you're in no box, you're in no category, your past doesn't define you, and how academic (or not) you are doesn't define how successful you'll be.

So let's go on a little journey together, hold on tight – it's gonna be a bumpy ride…!

YOU WON'T BE *everyone's* CUP OF TEA SO ADD *sugar, syrup* OR DRIZZLE *whatever* MAKES YOU, *you.*

SIMPLE PRETTY IN PINK EYES TUTORIAL

(My favourite everyday makeup look for summer)

STEP 1

Always start with your daily SPF moisturizer. I love using a filter finish base application to add a fresh glow to my skin (adding that glow before foundation makes your skin look super hydrated).

STEP 2

Dab a sheer foundation onto your skin. Then I love to go in with loose powder using either a super-soft powder brush or powder puff (focus on under your eyes and on your chin and forehead). Using loose powder is a great way to define your contour.

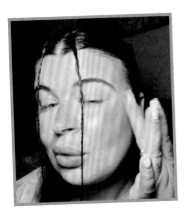

STEP 3

Apply baby pink blush to the temples and high cheeks (remember to use a large fluffy brush to disperse the product evenly, as we don't want our blush to be too harsh).

STEP 4

A tiny bit of highlighter goes the longest way, make sure to properly melt the highlighter into your skin. My top tip is to use a small fluffy brush and a loose highlighter.

STEP 5

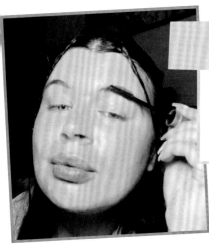

Use a brow gel through the brows to sculpt and add shape (our brows shape our face so styling them is so important).

STEP 6

Now onto the eyes! Spray a flat eyeshadow brush with setting mist, then dab into a light pink shimmer eyeshadow and apply to your lids (super simple but super effective).

27

STEP 7

Now go in with a white shimmer and apply to the inner corners of your eye (this will open your eyes up).

STEP 8

It's mascara time! If you want thicker lashes use a little bit of translucent powder to thicken the mascara up or use false lashes – you can even cut them in half for a cute foxy eye. Creating shape with the eyes can lift the face.

STEP 9

I'm currently obsessed with a tinted lip oil as they look not only natural but they are so hydrating for lips! You can always pop lip oil over your favourite matte lipstick for a glossy look.

STEP 10

Finally, spritz your face with a vitamin C face mist and make sure you use a fan to dry (this is so your makeup doesn't run). Using setting mist between your makeup layers is also a good little tip if you want long-lasting makeup.

HOW DOES THE FINAL LOOK
MAKE YOU FEEL? HERE'S
HOW MINE TURNED OUT!

STYLING

Let's open your wardrobe with a cuppa and chat before we start. I'm no professional stylist but you definitely don't need to be.

I'm a big fan of basics and adding structure to the body with simple looks such as flared trousers which add shape and complement any body type.

Then we have colour and patterns. I'm a big fan of monochrome zebra print which is bold and looks great against plain colours.

Then you've got to think about textures, which can be super important. For example, I wouldn't wear a satin dress with a wool jumper, instead I'd wear faux fur.

We all need to clear out our wardrobe from time to time and I know that it can be super overwhelming, so here is some food for thought:

♥ Keep your basics
♥ Keep your bold patterns
♥ Keep clothing which makes a whole outfit

Anything which no longer fits, no longer makes you feel good and no longer represents your style, let's put in a bag and drop it off at your local charity shop.

BODY POSITIVITY VS BODY CONFIDENCE

Time for a buckle-in moment – it's important to realize that true body positivity means ALL body shapes, not only those that are seen in media, advertising and fashion. In no way am I promoting unhealthy eating habits here – my message is to make people feel confident in their own body, and that's what body **POSITIVITY** is all about.

Then we have body **CONFIDENCE**, which is how you see your own body and how beautiful you feel in your own skin.

To help build my own body confidence, I love grabbing a red lipstick and writing a positive word about myself on my mirror every time I jump out the shower, wear a bikini or see my body. This really helps in times when I feel like I can't take on the world.

I also want to touch on body **INCLUSIVITY**, which means our weight, size, skin colour or any other diverse characteristics – these should all be included. So many brands claim to be body positive but still don't cater for certain body types. There are still so many people who aren't being represented.

We've got to learn to love our own bodies – I have realized in my lifetime that some of the most toxic body shaming that I've experienced are the critical negative comments I tell myself.

TAKE A SEAT AND ASK YOURSELF, WHAT IS BEAUTY?

If I got asked this 10–15 years ago, I would've pointed at the girls in every fashion magazine and told you that's beauty right there. However, I've now learned that the girl in the magazine isn't even real. We've been brainwashed to feel insecure, too small, too big and never good enough by advertizing campaigns, so that we buy more beauty products and spend money on 'perfecting' ourselves in the hope we look like that girl in the magazine, who isn't even real!

It's a lot to wrap your head around and I want you to know that exactly **THE WAY YOU ARE** is perfect, it's more than enough, and beauty is in the eye of the beholder. That's what makes us so unique and beautiful.

So, before you compare your beauty to someone else's, we're going to start by saying, "A flower doesn't compare itself to the flower it's blooming next to." We need to appreciate our body and all it does for us. Your body is a unique piece of artwork – it's made to protect you, it's your vessel which gets you through life. Love your body, it's incredible!

BAD days
are part of a
GOOD Life.

MY STAMMER

We all look and sound different but there is still so much stigma around hidden disabilities. I experience this a lot, especially when I'm having days where my stammer is less obvious.

There's nothing I want more than for everyone to realize that nobody is turning on and off or faking a disability, so please **PLEASE** never make anyone feel disrespected or belittled.

I mean, would you ever ask someone where their epilepsy, diabetes, anxiety, arthritis, post-traumatic stress disorder, autism, or hearing loss is? I'd hope not, so that's why I get frustrated when people do when it comes to a speech impediment.

DID YOU KNOW...?

Kindness has been shown to increase not only self-esteem but also empathy, compassion and your mood. It can decrease stress hormone levels and it benefits everyone involved. What random act of kindness will you do today?

Different kinds of kindness we can share:

- ♥ Leave a kind note in a library book
- ♥ Donate something to charity
- ♥ Bake something for your neighbour
- ♥ Leave a kindness rock at the park (a rock with a super cute message left on it!)
- ♥ Buy flowers for someone
- ♥ Donate food to a food bank
- ♥ Give someone a compliment
- ♥ Text a friend to let them know you're thinking of them
- ♥ Tell someone you love them
- ♥ Give a free hug
- ♥ Write someone a letter
- ♥ Leave a kind chalk message on the pavement
- ♥ Hold open the door for someone

GIRL, HAVE YOU GOT FIVE MINS?

Let's be childish. Chuck on that cha cha slide, get dancing, do the worm, see how many chocolate pieces you can fit in your mouth, play hide and seek or prank a family member.

My point is: these years of your life are stressful and society puts so much pressure on us to be **PERFECT** when true perfection doesn't even exist. Allowing yourself to let go, live in the moment, laugh and be silly helps me to remember what is truly important in life and that is all of the **LITTLE THINGS**.

COLD WATER THERAPY

Brrrrr-illiant idea if you love the cold but if not, hear me out ... cold water therapy is powerful for anyone struggling with their mental health. Today we're gonna do a cold water face bath which will not only give you the best looking skin, but make you feel like a fresh daisy who has just been reborn.

STEP 1

Grab yourself a pretty decent bowl with enough space to dunk that face in.

STEP 2

Run the tap until it's ice cold and fill the bowl up. Now plop in a handful of ice cubes. You want this to be **ICE COLD, BABY!**

STEP 3

Get a towel at the ready, because you're gonna submerge your entire face into this bowl. Dunk your face into the water for 10–15 seconds.
Do this 4–5 times for best results.

STEP 4

Enjoy that freshly reborn feeling! You are in total control of your mind, body and soul, and this is a great way to start the day.

SPRING BODY CONFIDENCE!

Now, every year when spring arrives all I want to do is carry on wearing my oversized layered outfits that cover every inch of my skin. I used to constantly compare myself to everyone else who was looking cute in little springtime pastel outfits.

I WANT YOU TO REALIZE THAT WHOEVER INVENTED AIRBRUSHING RUINED MANY LIVES AND WHOEVER AIRBRUSHES THEIR IMPERFECTIONS IN THIS MODERN AGE IS SADLY ADDING TO THE PROBLEM WE ARE TRYING SO HARD TO ESCAPE.

So, to start loving your spring outfits, I want you to grab some pastel water-based paint, a little paintbrush and a cuppa. Now go sit in the garden where the sunshine can beam down on your face and paint little pastel flowers all over your legs and arms.

I want you to realize that your body is a masterpiece and airbrushing any flaws is stripping away your individual unique piece of artwork. Airbrushing your body for online approval is being a copy-and-paste version of the girls in the magazines who, most of the time, aren't even real themselves.

I want you to take a photograph of the part of your body which you're most conscious about showing, covered in these pastel flowers. Upload it to social media using our hashtag #LetsTalkWithJessie to join our little community of incredible people just like yourself who are learning to love and respect their bodies.

STYLING FOR SPRING!

I'm sure you can agree that it's exhausting keeping up with fashion trends. That's why I prefer to focus on dressing for my body shape using basics that never go out of fashion, plus it's a more sustainable way to build a wardrobe.

So, let's build an outfit together for spring.

Monochrome basics are a dream, so first I'm going to take my black flared trousers and a basic tee. I like to think of my clothes as a pizza base and the accessories as the pizza toppings.

My mac coat is great to help layer this outfit up as the material is super light, it looks trendy and will keep the chill off.

I love to add in silver jewellery, and a bold chunky heart necklace is perfect when matched with silver hoop earrings.

You might know that I'm a lover of hats, so I'll add my leather beret and finish this look off with a chunky studded belt, black studded handbag and chunky boots.

Here is my outfit which might not be everyone's cup of tea but I hope it makes you realize how amazing basics can be, while also being dressed up.

43

LETTING GO

Right now we're all about **LETTING GO**. I don't care if it's letting go of stress or letting go of hoarding a dress. Our goal is to feel free. I'll go first.

STEP 1

Run down to the charity shop and pick up a cheap old plate. Then grab a permanent marker (or paints or anything else that you can use to write with on the plate).

STEP 2

Write down on your plate any things that make you feel rubbish and that you want to let go of. I've got loads of things on my plate, one of them being JEALOUSY. I'm letting go of comparing myself to everyone online. Side challenge: I'm also going to unfollow or mute anyone who makes me feel pants about myself because I'm having no pity party, you should try this!

STEP 3

Now we're going to put this plate inside a carrier bag. Tie it up tight and, in an open space outside, throw this at this ground, releasing all of your emotions as you allow the plate to smash.

FRIENDSHIPS

There is something about being popular in school that attracts **EVERYONE**, but as I've grown older I wish I could tell younger Jessie that being popular means quantity not quality. That's the truth and, without being disrespectful, friends often come and go – it's not uncommon for you to grow apart in life.

We are our own little boats on our own journeys, meeting fellow sailors on the way, but I also have my personal boat crew, my day-one girlies who are more like my soul sisters. We listen, talk, party, cry and understand each other with the most important quality being "expect nothing". That's what keeps our friendship so strong throughout our lives. We don't expect **ANYTHING** materialistic from each other. We don't expect each other to jump over mountains and rivers, and sometimes we can go weeks or months without talking or seeing each other, but we know at the end of the day we're always at the end of the phone when we need to be. That quality in a friendship is so hard to find, as people can often take friendships for granted. Imagine a game of tug of war, if one side keeps on take, take, taking, eventually the other side will fall. The same theory applies to a friendship: you gotta give as much as you take to be a good friend.

I want to take this moment to thank the girls in my life who have never seen my stammer as a disability but as a force of strength to be recognized. They never made fun or took my stammer as a weakness. These girls are my cheerleaders, and having a strong little friendship group is so important as we go through life. Finding true friendship is **RARE** but you'll vibe and feel an energy around certain people and these are the ones you wanna build a bond with.

Rose forever has her arms ready to catch me – I fall a lot and deeply when I'm mentally in a dark place. She's that friend who's my mother hen with comfort food at the ready to cheer me up. I feel so proud of all that she's overcome, especially her speech at my wedding which tackled her fear of public speaking. She was inspired by my speaking challenges and every word she said was straight from the heart. My eyes filled with oceans of happy tears.

Louise has the kindest, most beautiful soul I've ever seen. Nothing is ever too much of a problem and she is always there with her pom poms cheering me on through life. She even changed my shoes about 2,000 times on my wedding day from crocs to heels and back again. She's a real-life angel to me.

Leah is the warmth of the sun. The deep messages, quotes and love is like no other. When I started my TikTok journey I had my first experience with trolls, which made me wanna give up. She would always say to me, "Did Ed Sheeran give up? No, and now he sings to millions." Leah, you are my older soul sister in this life and I'm forever proud of you. True beauty comes from within, and yours shines like the first day of spring.

Dani is the party bus and if I ever need a party planned she's on it before we can even talk about balloon colours. She knows how to party and will make sure we plan or organize something so we have a get together. She's got a heart of gold and nothing is ever too much to ask.

These are the girls who saw me marry my best friend and cried tears that could fill a river. I never want to forget how lucky I am to have friends that have been through life with me.

ANXIETY TOOLBOX

Imagine if we could see anxiety. Imagine if it just appeared on our hand when we were anxious, or became something that we could switch on or off.

Sadly it's invisible, but it can show signs through our body, behaviour and mood. Hand on my heart, I grew up thinking it was normal to feel the way I did. So I feel, as your big sis, it's important for me to let you know it's okay to feel anxious sometimes, and it will come and go like a wave.

Firstly, get a shoe box or a container and fill it with thoughtful items that mean something to you or bring you inner peace. The shoebox is filled with things that bring you serotonin (a chemical in your body that makes you feel happy): a face mask, a note from a bestie, polaroid pics. Anything that brings you joy, in one place, where you won't lose anything.

Secondly, let's look at our breathing. Super obvious, I know, and I used to eye roll at this but believe me if you do it right, it's like a superpower. It's known as the 5-5-5 rule. Breathe in for 5 seconds, hold your breath for 5 seconds, then breathe out for 5 seconds, and continue until you start to relax.

I live by writing lists and writing down how I'm feeling. I find it helps to figure out what's making me feel the way I do and the root of my anxiety, but also sometimes we can be anxious for no reason whatsoever! It might just be your body's hormones that day.

Find out what makes you relax, and that doesn't always mean chilling on the sofa with a cuppa, it could mean doing some artwork, self-talk (see pages 104–105), puzzles or singing your favourite anthem in the car. It can be whatever you enjoy doing in life.

Take a break from social media, it will still be there tomorrow. You aren't missing out, trust me.

Remember when you feel anxious to connect with your support network and speak to someone who you feel comfortable with about how you're feeling.

I want you to know that anxiety affects almost 30% of adults at some time in their life, and its okay to struggle with it, just please know that there's so much help and support out there.

On page 144 is a list of helpful websites and organizations you can call if you need some support.

HYDRATION

Okay, confession time: I'm not a water lover. I definitely don't drink enough but, after looking into the importance of hydration, I've upped my daily water intake. Here's what made me realize water is incredible stuff:

- ♥ 60–70% of your body is water.
- ♥ Water keeps your body functioning and regulates your body temperature.
- ♥ Your joints are cushioned and lubricated by water.
- ♥ This blew my mind – water helps prevent infections and keeps our organs functioning properly.

I know I sound like your mother or teacher so I do apologize, but this is such important information I wish I knew growing up, and even as an adult **I HAD NO IDEA!**

I struggled daily with concentration, my mood, headaches and having energy. Honestly, filling up a cute, aesthetically pleasing water bottle and carrying it everywhere like a puppy with a new toy massively helped me to up my water intake.

YOUR SPACE REFLECTS YOUR MIND

Just thinking about the word "tidying" drains my energy like a five-mile bike ride, so instead I like to call it a "reflection of my mind".

Right, come on then, find your favourite song and chuck it on. Grab a recycling bag and let's start with the floor. Work your way up to the top of the room and finish with hoovering and dusting the cobwebs away. Set a timer for an hour and then **STOP!**

So, now the hour is up, how do you feel? Don't forget to finish off this activity by spraying your favourite scent or lighting your favourite candle.

The reason why we are tidying our space is so we can have a better night's sleep, but also have a clearer mind and focus on what matters most. Your space reflects your mind, remember!

TUMMY ROLLS

It's very bizarre when someone comments on another person's body. Everyone is different – some people struggle to gain weight whilst others struggle to lose it and some, no matter what they do, will always be the same weight.

To me it's like someone comparing hair growth. It's not a competition and shouldn't matter. Now I'm not saying your health doesn't matter, because we all need to nourish our bodies, eat a balanced diet and exercise regularly, but don't you think comparing our bodies and tummy rolls to a stranger online is bizarre?

Tummy rolls are completely normal. I used to think having a flat stomach meant when you sat down you had no rolls. That was my goal which was so ridiculous, as **EVERYBODY** has a tummy roll sitting down.

I'm splurging all this out like an over-filled trash can because I don't want you to focus on comparing your body. Focus on being healthy and fit but never compare. As a teen I thought my life purpose was to lose weight. I wish I had an older sister to tell me that to be loved you don't need to be a certain size. You're worthy of love no matter what number is on your clothing label.

Focus on your growth, manifestation, future and self love. If you are struggling please seek help from a professional.

MEMORY JAR

Do you know what I did when my phone broke? I had a tantrum, which if a neighbour had witnessed it would've looked like I was having a corker of a time listening to heavy metal music, but no, I was so mad. All my memories now gone, vanished because I lived my life through pictures, and my only memories were saved on my phone.

Get comfy, chuck that cushion behind your back, and find a nice groove, 'cause today we're making a memory jar. Our future self will thank us for this (trust me) and at the end of the year we can open the jar and unfold all our beautiful moments in life.

So, grab yourself a large jar, some pretty colourful card and a few nice felt-tip pens. Now here is where it gets magical: every time you see, hear, feel, smell, taste or experience something magical, write it down and put it in this jar.

For example, it could be a conversation, a feeling, good news, new food you've tasted, a goal you've achieved, or anything positive which can or can't be photographed.

Like I said, your future self will thank you for this as you re-live all the highlights which you would've probably forgotten to take a picture of, and you can't photograph a compliment!

my Soulmate!

Little girls often dream of being swept off their feet in a fairy-tale ending with the credits rolling and tissues at the ready!

Did I ever want to be a princess? **NOPE.** As a little girl I was obsessed with kicking a football around or playing on my mini skateboard which was lilac with little decal sweets, and much too focused on perfecting my side fringe which I trimmed every Friday in geography with a fellow fringe focused girl. It was a skilful art to master the perfect side fringe, may I add.

I was not interested in getting married and I believed nobody would ever love me due to my stammer. Boys in school mocked me and saw me as a target to make themselves look like the funny class clown, so why would I want to fall in love with anyone who's ready to make me their next joke?

So, how did I meet my soulmate and get my happy ever after end credits rolling in life, I hear you ask?

Ugh, I **HATE** to say it but social media brought us together and very drastically he got promoted from the position of mutual friend to being a real friend, BIG thanks to his hairstyle. I appreciate a good fringe when I see one. After many weeks of speaking online daily, it was time to meet and I had never fancied anyone so much, so the thought of stammering in front of him was making the backs of my knees sweat. I wished I had a fairy godmother who would just allow me to speak like a normal person just this one time.

We met and this is how I knew I was going to marry him within the first ten minutes of meeting him ... picture the scene: it's raining and I typically haven't brought a coat because I'm sweating profusely about stammering. He takes off his coat (yes, like from a movie) and gives it to me. He then only allowed me to walk on the inside of the pavement. He said "If a car mounts the curb it will hit me and you'll be safe."

When I stammered he never laughed, made a face or questioned it. My stammer wasn't taking the spotlight or being the entertainment. It was invisible to him and he saw me as Jessie the person, not the stammer. The feeling of being seen and heard and falling in love was new to me. I fell head over heels for a boy, not for what he ever said, but for how he made me feel. For a 16-year-old boy he was rare, one of a kind. On the day we met we wrote our names with a purple pen on a bridge pillar and suddenly I was his girlfriend and it felt like I was living in my own fairy tale.

Relationships are not easy and shouldn't be easy, however, the day he moved 100 miles away I felt my heart was made of glass and had now shattered. I knew this was the beginning of the end. No matter how many calls or texts we made to each other, in-person quality time is key. How can you love someone for seven years and feel complete without them by your side? But we made a promise that once a month we would be reunited. Looking back this was **THE TEST** that every relationship needs to go through to see if both of you are truly life partners.

The day we moved in together felt like a sunflower bridge being folded out over a sky blue river. That feeling of pure joy, those are the moments in life that are the highlights.

In 2017 my best friend in this entire world decided to get down on one knee and propose whilst sat in a car park on a cloudy spring day in March. It was my birthday and at the time, I was shocked, asking myself where's the balloons, flowers and confetti, like how every girl envisions it? As your big sis, all I'm gonna say is that all that materialistic proposal stuff doesn't matter when you've found love so rare that you live in your own fairy tale.

I coughed up hair balls every time I got asked when the wedding would be, especially as the years went on. I was **PETRIFIED** of saying my vows. A special moment in life with all our loved ones watching, and

I can't even tell the coffee barista my name. So we ended up being engaged for five years with the addition of our fur baby, Mimi, who's a sassy little diva of a pug who will lick clean your whole hand if you give her a biscuit.

Quickly moving on and it's 2022, the year of our elegant but quaint wedding which took place on our 12th anniversary. After nine months of working on my speech and building my confidence up to say my vows, it was finally the day that I shone like the 4th of July. The man who was once just a teenage boy with a glorious fringe is standing at the end of the aisle, waiting for me. **YES**, I was 40–45 minutes late, but we love a tradition right? I won't bore you with the details but yours truly spoke loud and proud and smashed her vows. Every word was said with love and confidence. This was my biggest

speaking challenge yet, which was then shared with the millions of followers who witnessed my progress over my journey. I never want a fellow stammerer to ever worry about falling in love and getting married ever again.

I ask myself daily: why did I allow my stammer to prevent me from finding love, accepting love and getting married? The answer is self-doubt. We don't all believe that we deserve whatever it is we want in life and in my life, love life and career I have always carried this baggage that's more than the allowed 22kg limit called **SELF-DOUBT**.

Open your arms, open your heart and open your mind. Your soulmate will love your perfections and imperfections. And never be afraid to be your original authentic self when finding love.

EMOTIONS

It's another grab-a-cuppa-brew kind of chat as we talk about emotions and what I wish someone told me a long time ago!

Firstly, find someone you trust to connect with and express your emotions and feelings to. To this person you will never be oversensitive, over dramatic or too emotional. A problem shared is a problem halved, right?

Secondly, negative emotions will eat away at you like maggots eating away at an old piece of fruit. Don't let this happen!

Thirdly, our bodies hold onto any negative energy, and we hold, wear and carry it round with us within different parts of our body. This means you can find yourself feeling achey, your tummy might be twisted up or your neck might feel really stiff.

Finally, imagine your friend telling you that they were feeling the way you feel, what would you say?

We've got to figure out why and how we're feeling the way we do by finding the seed, the root of that emotion.

So, what would be your advice to your friend who felt this way? And who is that person you trust enough that you'd ask them to do **"THE CHECK"** when you're on your period? You know the one.

Just remember: every feeling and emotion you feel is **VALID!**

EXPRESS HOW YOU'RE FEELING HERE
GO GRAB THAT PEN!

STYLING FOR SUMMER

Are you like me, forever saying "I have nothing to wear" but actually overwhelmed and unsure how to put a trendy-wendy outfit together?

So let's do this together right now. Chuck on the summer anthem that gets ya booty shaking side to side and body popping like a glow stick cause we're gonna donate any clothing that isn't serving us this year's summer sass.

Every year my style changes so I highly recommend investing in a timeless capsule wardrobe where all you gotta do is switch up your accessories.

Think of yourself as a pizza and your accessories as the toppings which can be switched up. Grab those headscarves, sunglasses, butterfly hair clips, necklaces, and headbands which will work for your base wardrobe, and trust me you'll be less overwhelmed when trying to find something to wear in the morning.

I'm a sucker for pastel colours in the summer time so I have a beautiful lilac puff sleeve dress which never goes out of style. I love to pair this with platform white sandals and a lime green satin headscarf for a girlie day out **BUT** I can make this dress also look formal for a meal by layering a jacket over the shoulders with a pair of heels and a low slicked back bun.

Remember, it's all about the **STYLING**, you do **NOT** always need new clothes!

HEALING ROCKS!

We all know **HEALING** is not pretty or easy and I am trying to heal many parts of myself from traumatic events in my life.

Today we're gonna take a trip to a lake, pond, the sea or any body of water, and we're going to let go of all the negative daily thoughts we have and consume about ourselves.

I want you to grab a non-toxic permanent marker and some rocks or pebbles that you feel gravitated towards and take a seat.

Take a minute and think to yourself, what are those daily negative thoughts that niggle away, the inner voice, that horrible version of you inside your mind? Write those thoughts down onto these pebbles.

On my rocks I often put "not being good enough", "anxiety", "failure" and "unworthy" as these are my daily negative thoughts.

I always feel like I am **NOT GOOD ENOUGH** as a wife, as a friend, as a dog mum, as a content creator, as a driver, as a makeup artist. Whatever it is, I'm not good enough.

ANXIETY can take over my thoughts and hold me back from enjoying myself. I was once invited to a Galentine's party with many other girls and at first I freaked out like, "Nope, I'm gonna sit this one out," but why should I?! Anxiety, you suck, and **I'M GOING!**

FAILURE haunts me every day, I work 18 hours a day and burn myself out in order to not be a failure. I mean I'm here right now writing a book still feeling like a failure so this has gotta go. What more do I need to do in order to feel **NOT** like a failure?

We've come to **UNWORTHY**, and every day I truly feel not worthy of my amazing husband and my incredible friends, and I guess that all comes under not feeling good enough. I need to realize my **WORTH**, so that's why this has gotta go!

So now we've got our negative thoughts on our rocks we are gonna **LET THEM GO!** I want you to put all your emotional and mental energy into this otherwise it won't work. So grab those rocks, look at the words, then with emotion **THROW** them into the water and feel that energy leaving you! How are we feeling now?

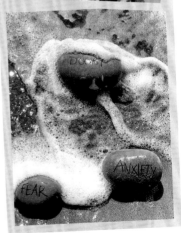

HOW YOU SPEAK TO YOURSELF MATTERS...

Talk and act like someone who feels good, positive and happy, and you'll attract all of that. Speak and act negatively with a life full of drama and gossip and you'll attract all of that, too.

What we speak, think and feel is top priority. The universe is listening and what goes around also comes around. Yes, you might have heard it all before but it's my biggest big sis advice.

Remember when I spoke about friendships, our circle and how it's so important? Our friends influence us and the way we think, which then impacts our lives.

A life full of peace and happiness is all we want but we've got to know how who we surround ourselves with will affect that.

BEING SELFISH

This word used to make me wanna scream. Every time I heard "you're so selfish" I would feel like the villain, as I was brought up to think that selfishness was a bad thing.

As I'm getting older, I thrive off being selfish. Selfish with my time, love and boundaries.

Being selfish doesn't have to be a bad thing. Well, if you're stopping a friend from eating a piece of your birthday cake, we're not on the same page. Sharing is caring in that aspect, but being selfish with **WHAT YOU WANT** out of life is a different story. I feel this comes hand in hand with the art of saying **NO.**

Being a people pleaser all my life, I found that saying yes brought uncomfortable situations I could have avoided if I had just said no. You're allowed to say no if you don't wanna do something and it's important to practise that. If a stranger asked you to go in their car, what would you say? If you've said yes, I need to let you know that you're putting yourself at risk and saying no protects us.

The same rules apply with life and being invited to events, situations, your career and life in general. Don't be afraid to say no when it is best for you.

GRATITUDE

This is a big sis chat moment and right now I'm gonna sound so clichéd so I wanna apologize but every morning on the way to school, college, gym, work or anything else you're doing, I want you to ask yourself, "What am I grateful for today?"

Trust me, the minute you become grateful and count your blessings, you'll start to see the good in everything. Realizing your blessings will bring so much value and happiness to your life. Like I said, it sounds so clichéd, but think about it – we're alive, breathing, drinking a morning cup of coffee. There's so much to be grateful for in life and all of the materialistic things won't go with us once our time is over in this world. So I'm gonna ask you again, "What are you grateful for today?"

Hear me out 'cause I love this activity. I want you to take a dry-wipe marker or some lipstick and draw some hearts on your bedroom, bathroom or living room mirror. Wherever you look daily to see your reflection, it **NEEDS** to be there. Write in each heart something that you're grateful for. For me, it's my family, friends, home and love.

73

REACTING VS RESPONDING

Let's be honest, life can be testing but people can also test us. Part of our self-growth journey is learning the difference between reacting vs responding.

Reacting is when you respond to a situation with an immediate and emotional reaction. Instinct and learned behaviour takes over which comes from a place of fear and allows no second thought for the outcome. It comes from an insecure place.

Responding requires you to re-evaluate and slow down. You become aware and can properly gauge your emotions and feelings and select your response, coming from a place of love and respect. Maintaining your self-control can help to reduce triggered or knee-jerk reactions. This comes from a place of feeling secure.

This is something I wish someone had told me years ago, as it has helped me massively with my self-growth and how I respond to situations in life.

Here's some great ways to reply to a friend who's upset you or a situation that has frustrated you:

♥ Use statements beginning with "I" and try and use neutral language, such as "I felt hurt when you…" or "I was frustrated that … happened."

♥ Try and explain how you would prefer the situation to be handled if it happens again. For example, "In the future, I would appreciate it if you would talk to me privately if you're upset with me.

I hope you find these tips as useful as I do!

5 THINGS I WISH I KNEW SOONER:

♥ IF IT WON'T MATTER IN FIVE YEARS DON'T SPEND MORE THAN FIVE MINS THINKING ABOUT IT. Very clichéd but very true!

♥ Comparison is the thief of joy, so stop comparing yourself to others, or you will always be unhappy.

♥ Celebrate little wins. Who can turn down a little celebratory dance?

♥ It is OKAY to ask for help.

♥ Take just five minutes a day to take care of yourself, like you would for someone you really love.

SELF WORTH

I'm gonna come out and say it ... can we please stop this "I did it, so can you" mentality? Not everyone has the same environment and support system and the reality is: nope, not everyone can, if I'm gonna be brutally honest. There is a sprinkle of luck involved 'cause nobody is in the exact same situation in life. I really hate generic inspirational books, ughhh it makes me roll my eyes and want to clap with cow manure in my hands. It's usually full of the same stuff I can find on Google when I search for a clichéd quote, which makes me feel good for 3–4 seconds but the truth is: grit and determination is more than just a quote and a "you can do it, because I did" approach.

What I will say is, you can be the right package at the wrong address. Repeat that. We're gonna talk about **SELF-WORTH** here. We all get told at some point in our life that we're about as useless as the letter 'G' in lasagne.

Yup, if you're asking me to change the oil in my car, you are correct, I am that letter G (useless!), but I know what I bring to the table in other areas. Forget the "I can do it, so can you" behaviour and tell me:

- ♥ What do you bring to the table?
- ♥ What is your strength?
- ♥ How can you use your strength in life?

my youtube dream

Not many people know, but in 2016 I started my own YouTube channel showcasing makeup tutorials. I'll be honest, many people around me laughed when they found out, including people at the place I worked. Nobody believed in me, but I believed in myself.

I picked up that makeup brush every evening after work. Painting my face then editing out every time I stammered because I didn't believe that the world could have a stammering influencer. Life was good, I was rubbing shoulders with some of the biggest beauty influencers in the UK. I was invited to NYX events, L'Oréal PR trips, I was a beauty influencer and suddenly the people who didn't believe in me wanted to know how I did it. I told them, **"SELF–BELIEF, BABY!"**

However, I felt lost and I was tired of putting on a mask to blend in into a community and an industry who didn't yet showcase people like me. I was proud of my achievements but hiding who I truly was didn't feel like something to be proud of. I decided to stop it all because I was living a lie and carried on with my 9 to 5 job. I ended up becoming an influencer full time by accident the minute I decided to be myself.

Girl, being your true authentic original self can be difficult, but it will forever be rewarding. I never want you to think that you can't do something because you're not the same as everyone else. You will never influence the world by being just like it.

You WON'T INFLUENCE the world by BEING LIKE IT.

THE RELATIONSHIP YOU HAVE WITH YOURSELF IS THE LONGEST AND MOST IMPORTANT

Listen, we all want the biggest house and fastest car, but what about being rich in memories and our relationship with ourselves?

So firstly I want you to think about three ways in which you show how you **TRUST** yourself, and write these down in your journal. For me, honestly believing in myself, having a strong gut instinct and accepting myself for who I am are ways I show that I trust myself.

Secondly, write three examples of how you love yourself. For me, it's my values and what I stand by in life, loving my imperfections and being connected with my emotions.

Thirdly, think of three examples of how you treat yourself. Always try to treat yourself how you would treat others and be kinder to yourself as this sets the bar for how others will treat you. This can be in relation to your time, attention, uniqueness.

Last but not least, think of three examples of how you challenge yourself. If you follow my social media you will know I love to challenge myself daily as it develops not only my social skills and ability to speak to strangers or speak publicly, but the confidence to say, **"YUP, I CAN DO IT!"**

DON'T COMPARE YOUR TIMELINE TO SOMEONE ELSE'S TIMELINE

Your big sis checking in right now and I just basically wanna say that as a 30-year-old woman I have felt myself comparing my own timeline to many other people's timelines, even some of my best friends.

Yes, I feel the pressure to have it all figured out, to have children of my own, and to hit other milestones, but that doesn't come easy to everyone and right now all my friends have their own children and more on the way.

Basically, what I'm saying is, I know many of us feel the pressure to be in a relationship, hit milestones and keep up with whoever, but don't do anything until in your heart and soul you're ready.

I guess this is self-explanatory, but I wanted to mention this as I wish I had been told about this "Keeping up with the Joneses" mindset that can happen to us in life (where you compare yourself with others and struggle to keep up).

Stay in your own lane, drive at your own comfortable speed and don't let the people behind you make you feel you gotta speed up or change lanes.

THE TRUTH ABOUT YOUR CLOTHES

It's bizarre why I still have jeans, dresses and even pairs of underwear which are so much smaller than the size I currently am because I keep telling myself that one day I **WILL** fit back into these. I have now realized that clothes are supposed to fit **ME** and it's not **ME** that needs to fit into **CLOTHES**.

So let's declutter our wardrobe today. Grab a coffee, chuck on a feel-good tune and think of how amazing we will feel afterwards.

Slight detour – may I ask what your definition of beautiful is? Is it a rainbow? Is it a flower? Is it your favourite food?

WE ARE BEAUTIFUL. It isn't one single thing and I hope that you can see your own beauty. Often we can be so used to our own facial features that we don't realize it.

Right, let's get back to work and tackle this wardrobe.

Any clothes which are currently too big or too small we are giving to charity. My top tip is to keep any basics which fit you, as these can be worn throughout the year and mixed in with a bold colour or pattern.

Try to build an outfit on the hanger so you can grab and go. This makes getting dressed in the morning super quick and you don't have to use any mental energy.

EVENING MAKEUP TUTORIAL

If you're anything like me, getting dressed up and having a evening out is one of your favourite things to do.

STEP 1

ALWAYS prep the skin with a little cleanse, tone and moisturize and never forget that SPF. Then allow these products to sink in for about five mins.

STEP 2

Let's go in with eyes first, just in case we have any fall out. I love to use bronzer on my eyelids first, then dab on either loose glitter pigment or a liquid glitter gel all over the lid.

STEP 3

Next, go in with a fluffier lash than you might wear every day, I usually go for a fox eye wing lash to elongate the eye.

STEP 4

Time for brows! Use a brow gel to create shape and sculpt then go in with a powder or pomade to fill and define.

STEP 5

Now let's prime our faces. I love using a light illuminator to give my skin a little glow before applying our foundation.

STEP 6

It's personal preference with foundation but with tinted moisturizers, BB cream, full coverage and many more on the market to choose from, there's such a range for everyone.

STEP 7

Let's brighten our under eyes. I **LOVE** going in with a super light concealer under the eye in the inner corner then applying a concealer which is two shades darker to the rest of the under eye.

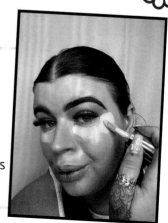

85

STEP 8

Depending on how snatched you like your contour, if you're looking for a light definition just use your contour powder, but if you love a defined, snatched face I prefer to use a contour cream stick **THEN** layer it with contour powder. Don't apply your contour too low, the higher the better as this will lift your face. I also apply my contour around my forehead, nose and chin and when blending, blend upwards. Top tip: if you spritz your setting mist after every step, your makeup should last all night long.

STEP 9

Now we need to secure all our cream products with a translucent powder. The best way to use a setting powder is to use a powder puff and apply a light layer **THEN** go in with a bake for long lasting makeup, this can also help define your face.

STEP 10

Blusher has become **HUGE** and I think we can all see why, as it's not only pretty but can perk up your complexion. Right now, baby pink blush is trending, but it's always changing. Apparently your perfect blush shade should match your natural inner lip colour.

STEP 11

This is my favourite step because highlighter for me changes your makeup and lifts your bone structure. Personally, I go for a golden shade as I don't want my highlighter to look grey or ashy. I also prefer to use a loose powder highlighter as the product just melts into the skin.

STEP 12

Time for lips. I always get asked about my lip combo and there's nothing I love more than a light brown lip liner which I use to line and also fill in my lips. Then I dab a nude matte lipstick into the middle of my lips. Finally I like to use a lip oil as a gloss, which keeps my lips super hydrated.

STEP 13

Never skip this final step, which is to apply setting mist. This will help blend your makeup together and make it last longer, whilst also hydrating your face.

FEAR OF LOOKING SILLY

I will be real with you here, the fear of looking silly is real, but it's holding you back! What would you do if NOBODY was watching you?

There is no doubt about it – society and other people's opinions have got us constantly doubting ourselves and wanting to blend in but that will never work in your favour. So let me just ask you: what do you want out of life?

- ♥ What would you want to wear?
- ♥ How would you live your life every day if you didn't have school or work?
- ♥ What would your future look like?

Now I want you to realize that all of the above can be possible when you stop caring and being influenced by society.

You're allowed to be a **WORK** *of* ART *but also a* work *in* PROGRESS

ANXIETY BEFORE A CHALLENGE!

Alright, we all know that we can't control what's gonna happen in any situation, and anxiety has the ability to make you worry about the worst case scenario. This can be an even stronger worry when facing a challenge for the first time.

I would feel like this every single time I challenged myself, however now I try to focus on the buzz afterwards and that feeling is something that money just can't buy. The feeling of being your own hero, being high on life and feeling the growth.

It's easy to focus on the nerves, anxiety and worry before a presentation, challenge, fear, interview, whatever it is, but I want you to focus on the **AFTER FEELING.**

Give answering these questions a go, so we can help change your mindset and how you tackle the fear of challenging yourself.

- ♥ When was the last time you felt incredible from a personal achievement?
- ♥ Why do you worry about the worst case scenario?
- ♥ Do you believe that personal growth starts from facing your fears?
- ♥ Why and how will you grow?

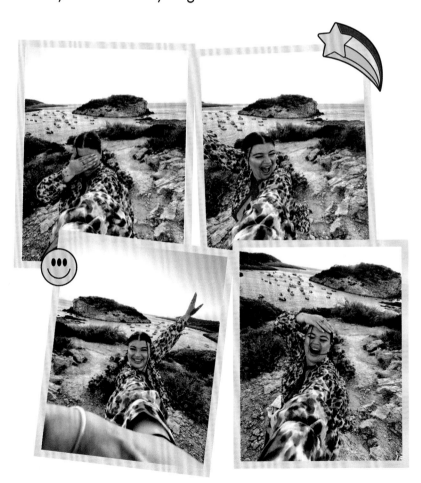

INNER HAPPINESS

I think it's time we talk about inner happiness, as it's very different to what we think it is. As a little girl I thought happiness was owning lots of handbags and shopping every day, I mean, that does make me happy, but that's not true inner happiness.

Firstly, you need to accept the journey you've been granted and learn the lessons that unfold. The biggest lesson that I've learned is that happiness doesn't come from someone else, it's simply found from within **YOU.**

Trust me, life can throw some rain clouds at you, along with a rumble of thunder, but don't forget to always look for the lesson and, as they say, every cloud has a silver lining.

Truth be told, happiness finds me in random moments throughout the day and then it goes again. These random moments could be when I'm singing my feel-good anthems from the top of my lungs. It could be when I'm walking on the sand barefoot.

Personally, I have found my true inner happiness comes easiest when doing the things I used to love as a little girl. I find so much joy in painting, swimming, going to the beach and riding a bike.

I've also realized how we gotta learn to accept the things we cannot control. My current favourite little daily saying is:

WHAT'S MEANT TO BE YOURS IS ALREADY MAKING ITS WAY TO YOU

STYLING FOR AUTUMN

Hands down let me tell you my favourite season is autumn, purely because I'm a girl who thrives off layering clothes. I'm someone who wears more layers than a trifle.

In autumn the classic brown, beige and green shades come into season, but never be afraid to venture outside of this. My personal favourite outfit is a pair of leather high waisted flares paired with a cropped white top and a snazzy inspector-looking mac coat. Don't forget accessories: a classic beret and chunky platform boots work perfectly for this look.

Also, you don't have to chuck that summer maxi dress in the attic just yet! Chuck on some tights, a long sleeve tee, a leather jacket with those platform boots and work it, girlie!

Trust me when I say: the BEST blazers I've ever bought are from a charity shop in the men's section, 'cause an over-sized blazer with jeans and a plain tee will forever be more iconic than a full English breakfast. P.S. why not try chucking a beige hoodie under your blazer and wack your hair in a slicked-back bun, just thank me later!

Oh and I CANNOT forget to mention my cute lil dog walking outfit: leggings, crop top, cap and a beige mac or a longline gilet. Don't forget that iced coffee in your hand!

95

COMPLIMENT A STRANGER

We all love a compliment in life, but fact of the matter is, giving them can be daunting and we often hold ourselves back.

That's why today I've decided it's time we do something outside of our comfort zones. Don't worry, I'm here to hold your hand and guide you through it all.

Okay, so you can literally compliment anything and everything. We can either say it verbally or we can just simply hand someone a written compliment.

Here are some examples, but feel free to make up your own:

- ♥ You are so kind.
- ♥ I'm so glad you're my friend.
- ♥ You've accomplished so much!
- ♥ I love your laugh.
- ♥ I trust you.
- ♥ Your confidence inspires me to be more confident myself.
- ♥ I love how I can be myself around you.
- ♥ That outfit looks amazing on you.
- ♥ Your hair is so beautiful.

So, maybe start off with a friend, or someone in your family. Then, maybe work up to a stranger. This could be someone you see in the street, someone behind the till at a shop, someone in the drive-through taking your order, **ANYONE**!

After the activity I want to know a few things:

♥ How did you feel before giving the compliment? Probably scared? Anything else?
♥ How do you feel now?
♥ Did it made you want to give out compliments again?

BE
BOLD

CLICHÉD MANIFESTING

I've called this part clichéd because honestly, I used to eye roll every time I heard "manifestation". It's like hearing, "Let's do magic."

However, once I got over the eye rolling and practised it daily I realized how powerful manifesting can be. Here's a good analogy to help you understand: when you start to imagine your favourite meal, do you start to imagine the smell and taste, and does your mouth start to water?

Visualizing and manifesting your future works in the same way, so let's grab a groovy pen and get to this.

What does your ideal future look like?

Once you've got the vision let's move on to how it makes you feel, and identify those emotions that you're feeling.

What can you hear?
What are you looking at and what can you smell?

Lock onto this vision and go back to it daily.

What you've just experienced is your manifestation, this will help with your mindset, decisions and how you respond to different paths in life.

FIVE THINGS YOU CAN DO TO HELP YOUR MENTAL HEALTH

I will put my hand up and openly say that I struggle with my mental health. A few factors which contribute to the quality of my mental health are self acceptance, adaptability, defence mechanisms, social connection and regulation. All human-specific cognitions.

So what does that mean you should do, I hear you ask. Well...

♥ Connect with people who care about your wellbeing and never judge you.
♥ Discover a hobby which makes you forget about real life and escape into your bubble.
♥ Live in the moment and not online. Social media will always be there tomorrow.
♥ Give to others – something as small as a compliment or a smile will shift the chemicals in your brain.
♥ Change your environment, fresh air outdoors with no distractions is ideal.

You've just gotta find what works for you. This could be going for a run in the pouring rain, screaming a song from 2001 on your own or sitting for a quiet five minutes on a bench with a nice view. Whatever it is, make time for you.

GROWING UP

Isn't it hard figuring out what you want from life, who you are as a person, what's the right thing for you and who's truly got your back?!

So here it is from your big sis. When you **GROW** you will **CHANGE!**

You are not the same person you were as a small child, never mind last year. We all change and that's okay. I have been told "you've changed" so many times since starting my journey and yes, correct, I used to be a people-pleaser with no boundaries.

The beauty of working on your personal growth is being more selfish with your time, people having less influence over you and realizing your worth. Boundaries are put in place to protect **YOU** because then people can no longer keep hurting you. Having boundaries is **HEALTHY**. The only people who will be offended are the ones who are used to controlling or hurting you.

Please remember that the people in your life right now might not always be in your life as you both grow and go your separate ways in life. That is completely normal and there is **NOTHING** wrong with you!

BURNOUT!

Grab a cuppa and pop your feet up for this one, as I just want to tell you that feeling burnt out and overwhelmed will probably happen to you time and time again unless your habits and mindset changes.

As cringe as this sounds, I like to think of myself as a car, yes don't laugh, but a car needs a service, MOT, tyre change, new parts and, if you're like me, a new air freshener every 14–21 days. The truth of the matter is that we need **BALANCE.**

You're probably asking where do I start and what do I do with this?

So firstly, instead of saying "I did nothing today" and feeling guilty that you didn't hang out with friends or complete your tasks from the forever building up list of things to do, write today in your diary that today was a **REST DAY FROM BEING THE QUEEN THAT I AM.**

Then you need to tell yourself that recovering from the week, having a mental health day, catching up on your favourite show, making time to do your skincare routine, having a well needed nap, self-reflecting, choosing to not make plans, or any other way you like to rest and relax, is **NEEDED.**

I can party like it's 1999 if I realize why having your MOT, service and air freshener changed is so important and it should absolutely not be seen as an **"I DID NOTHING"** day.

Let's do a little dance together right now if we're gonna start marking "the queen needs a rest today" in our diaries?

I guess I need to tell you this now so that you can see the bigger picture. Through my years I've seen the pattern of believing I'm a woman with more time, body parts and energy than anyone else, feeling overwhelmed, and then hitting a burnout zone. This then puts a dent into my mental health which has me howling like a werewolf on the phone to my nearest and dearest talking about how I want to quit my dreams and lay under the bed for six months along with the dust and darkness.

I never wanna hear you say "I did nothing" ever again, so now we've had this little chat, let's move on!

SPEAK TO YOURSELF

I heard about this activity months ago and at first it sounded silly, but then I saw the method to the madness.

So, grab a photo of your younger self and I want you to stick this onto a mirror. Every morning whilst you're doing your skincare routine or makeup, I want you to speak to this little person. What do you think about them, what are your hopes for them, are you proud?

After a few days, I want you to pop a picture of your current self on the mirror and speak to them.

Has your tone of voice changed and are you still talking to them positively?

What I want you to realize is that we need to start speaking to ourselves with positivity, as we will believe what we hear about ourselves even if it's coming from ourself.

Every morning, speak to these two people as if you were speaking to your idol in life. Realize that you are the writer and director of your own life, and positivity will lead to happiness!

BUCKET LIST

This list of the experiences, achievements or goals that you hope to have or accomplish during your lifetime is so important.

Write your bucket list RIGHT NOW!

The urgency to write your bucket list is so you have a focus and have a goal you want to achieve, otherwise we are just fish swimming along in the water current.

- ♥ Where do you want to visit?
- ♥ What do you want to experience?
- ♥ What do you want to achieve?
- ♥ What are you doing today that will get you closer to your bucket list being ticked?
- ♥ Which one do you want to tick off first?

BE RICH IN
Memories,
NOT things.

FEMALE BODIES

I was forever at war with my own body growing up, so I want
YOU to write all the things that you **LOVE** about your body
on the body shapes above.

We nit pick at our flaws every day which makes us blind
to how beautiful we truly are. If a negative thought comes
I want you to do the body painting activity on pages 40–41.
Your body is a masterpiece, and differences, what you might
consider as flaws, make you unique.

LAZY GIRL SUNDAY ROUTINE

Alright, there was a time where every Sunday evening I was one heck of an anxious girlie, forever questioning why I **FELT** so anxious for a Monday morning.

So, creating a very relaxing Sunday afternoon/evening ritual was a must. I will be honest, not every self-care ritual is going to work or feel the same, so it's good to be flexible. Some days I plunge my face into cold water and it works and other days I need to sit in a dark room listening to a thunderstorm for 20 minutes.

Let's start with lowering the lighting, as it's great to start with the ambiance. Put on some relaxing music, figure out what scent calms you down and pop that candle or oil diffuser on.

Let's map out each day of the week. This is so we can mentally plan what we have gotta do this week and what we need to achieve, which will hopefully settle our anxiety.

Another top tip is to start journaling before bed. It is a form of self-care. I like to write down my mood, current feelings, what's triggering me or what I'm excited about and looking forward to in life.

Now, before bed let's pop on an audio book or listen to relaxing sounds like rainfall, or read a book which will switch your mind off from what's happening in reality.

I gotta say, as someone who struggles to sleep, I **HAVE** to put my phone in a drawer, listen to natural sounds and focus on my breathing.

These are all things we often already know about, but forget to put into action so I hope this is a good reminder to focus on **YOU!**

ACCEPTING YOUR INDIVIDUALITY

For me, my stammer was always a curse. I was forever saying "why me?" and praying daily that I would wake up being able to speak like my friends. I just wanted to blend in with the crowd.

After many years I've realized that you can't influence the world by being like it, but I know that not following the crowd and going in a different direction is daunting.

Even now I'm still looking for another influencer with a stammer who's influenced millions, and the truth is there's never been one before.

That leads me to say that you will always be too much, not enough, too loud, too quiet. There'll always be something, but the secret is to just be your true, original, authentic self and your light will shine **SO BRIGHT!**

NOBODY IS THE SAME AS YOU, AND THAT IS YOUR POWER

MY CAREER AND ACCOMPLISHMENTS

Before my TikTok journey I had achieved things I didn't even think were possible so let's start with 2015: the year I finished my degree. I'm a student living paycheck to paycheck and the opportunity comes up to do a graduate art show in London, an exhibition which would include my work. At this time I declined, as I didn't have the funds to travel to London, never mind stay overnight. I remember sitting on the loo thinking, "Why am I throwing away this opportunity? If you keep saying 'no', when do you expect this career to start because nobody will come looking for you when the door is shut."

I decided in that moment on the loo that I **WAS** going to take part in the grad show. I booked the coach and stayed in the cheapest hostel. I walked to the exhibition every day for three days and on the last day went back home on the coach while my work was still on show at the exhibition.

When I got home the phone rang. Someone wanted to buy my work, then I got another phone call ... a photo agency in London loved my work and they wanted to sign me up to their company. I signed that contract and within weeks had my photographs published on book covers around the world. It was 2016 when the biggest opportunity ever came in, to have my photograph published on the front cover of a best-selling book which would get printed worldwide for a very well-known author. It was a moment that I will never forget. I saw my photograph on giant billboards, on the sides of buses, and in the most famous stores in New York City.

I felt like I was living in a dream and now I wanted to achieve my dream of moving to London to work as a photographer.

I joined a talent programme run by Nick Knight, a famous fashion photographer, getting feedback from people such as the editor of *Vogue*. I had my pocket full of dreams and attended an interview for my dream job as a photographer in London, once again travelling on the coach. I sat in front of my future employer who asked for my name. I then spent ten minutes trying to say the word, "Jessie". I had allowed my anxiety, self-doubt and stammer to steal the show, and I left the interview without being able to say my own name.

That was a turning point in my career, where I told myself you just gotta take the good with the bad but also the ugly, and the universe has a plan for you and that job was just not it.

I then decided to become a freelance wedding photographer. I was just taking the pictures, and this was what made me happy and fulfilled my soul. Yet still, my voice, my stammer, was my biggest enemy. I decided to get a job as a support worker and I guess I kinda gave up on myself. There's nothing wrong with being a support worker, it was the most rewarding job I have ever had but **I GAVE UP ON MYSELF.** I allowed my speech, my anxiety and my self-doubt to defeat me.

On the side I was doing my friends' makeup on a Saturday afternoon, which led to doing their friends, and so on, that was my only happy place. I felt stuck, it was groundhog day every day; my life was on repeat. I lost my sparkle, I lost Jessie.

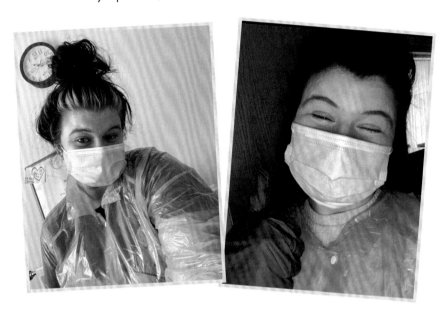

I had a YouTube channel doing makeup tutorials in order to find my sparkle but edited out every time I would stammer just so I could fit in. I won't lie to you, I was **GREAT** at hiding it. I went on a few trips, met other YouTubers but I was living a lie. I felt like such a fraud editing out my stammer, meeting people and trying so hard to not stammer. It eventually made me stop that path in life as I felt I needed to reflect on who I truly was and what I wanted from life, and that was not it.

In 2019, I had a mental breakdown. This was the type where you cry for hours. I cried all day, in work, in my car, to my fiancé, to everyone!

It was that moment in my life I realized that I needed a light, something to save me from drowning and I guess the support of millions and millions around the world saved me from myself.

I grew a community on TikTok and this has been my greatest achievement and the best journey I've ever been on.

It isn't about having your name in flashing lights, it's about how it makes me feel – the support, a community of strangers who provide a safety net and say they're here for you. Now go be **YOURSELF** because we **LOVE** you for **YOU!**

BODY HAIR

First things first, I want you to understand and realize that you will feel pressured by society but I want you to know that body hair is normal and it's **YOUR** choice if you want to shave it off. Please know it has nothing to do with your identity.

A cheeky little bit of history for you, the idea of being hairless came from the beauty and fashion industry but before, in the 1920s, women did not shave.

I've heard people say, "Ewww, so unhygienic," but it got me thinking, "Honey, men are covered in hair, so are they dirty?"

I remember when I was a teen and my body hair began to grow, and I had no idea what to do with it other than shaving 'cause all I'd hear the other girls say is "I haven't shaved my legs for P.E.," and that's how I was brainwashed into thinking I **HAD** to shave.

Just remember, it's a **CHOICE** and **YOUR** body so you do whatever makes you feel beautiful. Beauty isn't being hairless, it is when you feel yourself and that is **TRUE BEAUTY.**

IF ALL YOU DID

TODAY

WAS HOLD YOURSELF

TOGETHER,

≫ I am so ≪

PROUD

of you.

P.M. SKINCARE ROUTINE

Girl, lemme tell you, investing in your skincare is part of self-care, and in the long run it will pay off. It's great when you're being told that you look five years younger than you actually are!

So, allow me to share with you my night time routine:

STEP 1

We **ALWAYS** need to cleanse the skin. Even if you haven't been wearing makeup throughout the day, pollution builds up on your skin. So, invest in a cleanser for your skin type.

STEP 2

Now, we want to focus on using a toner as this will improve the appearance and tightness of your pores and balance out the PH levels of your skin.

STEP 3

Serum time! A normal part of skin maturing is developing fine lines and wrinkles, so don't worry too much about this happening. It happens to everyone at some point! But there are some serums that help your skin to look brighter and reduce any blemishes while also focusing on hydration and boosting collagen. You can also apply spot treatment in this step if you are prone to a breakout.

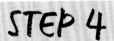

STEP 4

If you want to use retinol, it's important to apply before your moisturizer and only in the evening, as sunlight can diminish its strength. If using, only apply every other night. Retinol is used for aging and acne however do not mix retinol with vitamin C, benzoyl peroxide and AHA/BHA acids.

STEP 5

Moisturizing your skin is highly important, especially if you have dry skin. Using a nourishing night cream in your evening skincare routine works with your body's natural overnight recovery process.

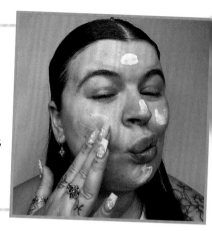

STEP 6

I won't lie, I used to skip this step, but now I realize how important applying eye cream to brighten dark tired-looking eyes can be. It also leaves your under eyes smoother, allowing your under eye makeup to look flawless.

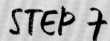

STEP 7

The last step is to use a face oil but my personal preference is to use a mist, as oils can be heavy on the skin. This final step is to lock in moisture and to feel refreshed.

Now to allow all these products to sink into the skin and work their magic! Don't forget, sleep also helps with your skincare as it repairs skin cell damage, so make sure to get those minimum seven hours!

DEAR JESSIE,

I WISH YOU SAW YOUR BEAUTY WHICH OTHERS SEE. I KNOW IT FEELS YOU ARE STILL AND STAGNANT RIGHT NOW, AND YOU'RE FEELING STUCK.

YOU'RE CONSTANTLY LOOKING SO FAR AHEAD INTO THE FUTURE, THAT YOU AREN'T APPRECIATING OR LIVING IN THE NOW. WHY DO YOU KEEP WISHING YOUR LIFE AWAY?

EVERYONE HAS THEIR OWN "HARD" IN LIFE, NOBODY HAS IT EASY BUT YOU ARE GOOD ENOUGH. DESPITE WANTING TO CRY RIGHT NOW YOU NEED TO REALIZE THAT YOU ARE A BEACON OF LIGHT FOR SO MANY. THE PEOPLE WHO AREN'T SEEING YOUR LIGHT DON'T DESERVE THE ACCESS THEY HAVE TO YOU. YOU ARE A HUMAN FULL OF EMOTIONS AND LIFE IS NOT A CONSTANT

HIGH, IT'S A ROLLER COASTER FULL OF DIPS AND TWISTS AND TURNS. KEEP FEELING AND LISTENING TO YOUR HEART 'CAUSE IT KNOWS WHAT'S BEST FOR YOU.

ALSO NEVER THINK YOU'RE ALONE. IT'S OKAY TO ASK FOR HELP, TO SAY NO AND TO ALSO REST. YOU ARE NOT FAILING, EVEN A CAR NEEDS A REGULAR SERVICE AND MOT.

LOVE YOU ALWAYS,

ME XOXO

TOP TIPS TO LIFT YOUR MOOD

1. Chuck on your **FAVOURITE** song

2. Grab a hair brush, mop or broom to sing into

3. Open those blinds or curtains and look up to the sky

4. **DO NOT** open any social media

5. Give your pet the biggest twirling hug ever

6. **DRESS UP** today. Wear something bold!

7. **SMILE** at anyone and everyone, and when they smile back take note of that feeling

8. Drink a tall glass of **WATER**

9. Take a 10-minute walk, this can release endorphins

10. Live every day being the main character, it's your story, your life

VISION BOARD INSPIRATION!

Ugh, nothing numbs my mind more than a boring canvas full of generic pictures of things people want to achieve. Show me emotion, how you would feel and sprinkle it with personality.

So, let's have a girlie **VISION BOARD NIGHT** with your bestie!

Grab those scissors and any newspapers and magazines that we have, and start cutting out letters and words for our board.

Personally I prefer my vision board to have a quote in the middle which will become my daily motto. For example, it could be:

"DON'T LIVE THE SAME YEAR 75 TIMES AND CALL IT A LIFE"
OR
"HOLD THE VISION, TRUST THE PROCESS"

First things first though, we should never lay our vision on a blank board or canvas. That ain't the right soil for your dream to grow on so I want you to get your aprons at the ready and tip, throw, spill or paint colour all over it.

Once that's dry, we can move to the next step. Now, I don't want a static stale image, I want words that represent the emotion and the feeling you will get when you achieve that goal on your vision board. That's what I want you to add.

Layer each word with even more colours and textures from the magazines, be creative in how you add the pictures of your goal. For example, if you want to travel around America, don't put the word "America" but instead put pictures of all the things that **MAKE** America and why you want to visit it. This could be a cactus, the food, hair in the wind as you cruise on the back of a motorbike. **GET CREATIVE** and get that **VISION** to **LIFE**, so brightly that you can taste and feel yourself there.

This vision board might be a one-day process or two-month process, as we're constantly adding to our vision board mentally as we go through life.

Now when your vision board is complete I would love to see it! Share on social media using our hashtag #LetsTalkWithJessie.

I look forward to seeing your vision and sending you all the luck in the world as your visions come to life.

NO
RAIN

NO
FLOWERS

WINTER STYLING

You know me, I am a **BASICS** girl, I really am. So what we're going to do now that the seasons are changing and our chills are multiplying, is we're gonna invest in an iconic statement **COAT!**

A few years back I purchased a monochrome zebra print coat which is always being complimented. She works so well with a cute monochrome accessory moment. Years on I still get asked about her! We spend so much time in a coat, and they should last for a long time, so get investing.

I would also say knee-high boots are crack-a-lacking for winter. Forget wellies, my angel, these will be your new best friend. Just make sure to also wear some super fluffy socks to keep those twinkle toes warm.

So, clothes-wise, go for that basic long-sleeved tee, flared trousers or wide leg jeans, oversized jumper, **BASIC**ally, the simpler the better.

Finally, accessories make me wanna jump higher than my 6ft 5in husband 'cause I **LIVE** for it. Your hat should always contrast the outfit, the bag needs to flow, that's why most of us stick to black, silver or white bags (except when your pink fluffy one just makes the whole thing POP!).

WRITE A GOODBYE LETTER AND BURN IT!

Are you struggling right now with something? 'Cause me too and I don't know about you, but I need these emotions, thoughts and feelings to leave.

All we need is paper and some cute felt pens and we're going to release all this negative energy by writing down what's bothering us right now in this present moment.

I'll go first...

Right now, I'm over-thinking about my public speech next month in London in front of hundreds of people. I'm also feeling nervous about the party tomorrow, where I'll meet new people. What if I stammer in front of them all? Will they like me, will they laugh, what if I'm left alone?

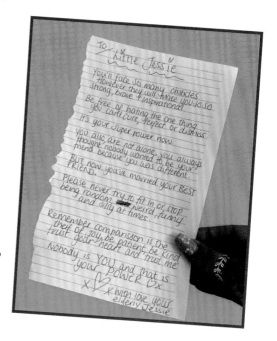

Yup, these are my thoughts right now, so I want you to do the same and have a think about the following questions:

- ♥ How are you feeling?
- ♥ What do you need to let go of?
- ♥ How do you want to feel?

Make sure you're not near anything too flammable for this next part (yes, including hair extentions!) as it includes a little bit of fire.

So, what we're going to do now is take this letter outside, and carefully set it on fire. When you watch it burn, take deep breaths and tell yourself, "I've got this, I'm incredible and I'm powerful."

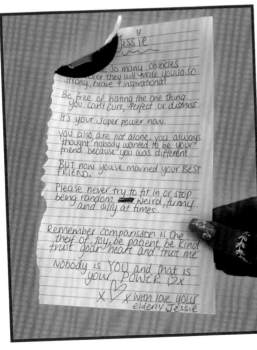

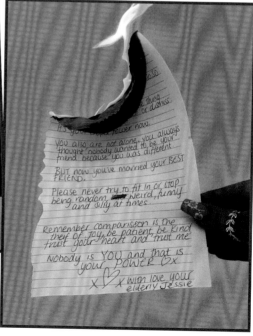

This book is proof that anything can happen in life!

I'd love to say the biggest and warmest thank you
to the darlings who follow my journey on TikTok
and made a small voice like mine so loud that
the world couldn't ignore it.

We may have over 1 billion views, but the fight to
end the stigma around stammers continues so please
donate if you can to my chosen charity Action for
Stammering Children as they help so many children
realize and understand that they've got a superpower
and it's nothing they should ever be shamed of.

If I could tell myself anything, it's to never think you've
got it all figured out or that this is the end, as the sun
always shines again even on your darkest day.

Last but not least, always be your:

TRUE, ORIGINAL, AUTHENTIC, RAW SELF

LOTS OF LOVE,
JESSIE

INDEX

USEFUL LINKS FOR FURTHER READING

Action For Stammering Children

ASC's mission is to ensure that every child and young person across the United Kingdom who stammers has access to effective services and support to help them meet the challenges created by their stammer.
www.actionforstammeringchildren.org

The McGuire Programme: Alternative Stuttering Therapy

The McGuire Programme is a global community of people who stutter dedicated to helping individuals who stutter overcome their challenges and gain control over their speech.
www.mcguireprogramme.com

Anxiety UK

Anxiety UK provides a wide range of free and paid anxiety courses and resources for those experiencing or supporting others with anxiety. They provide resources to support adults and children with a range of anxiety concerns, including stress, generalized anxiety, panic attacks and social anxiety. They organize regular support groups for those struggling with anxiety. You can call their anxiety helpline on 03444 775 774 or text 07537 416 905 for immediate support with anxiety.
https://www.anxietyuk.org.uk

Shout

A confidential and anonymous 24/7 text support service for anyone struggling to cope. It is free to text Shout from all major mobile networks in the UK. To speak to a trained volunteer, text SHOUT to 85258
www.giveusashout.org

Young Minds

Young Minds provides free online resources for support around a wide range of psychological concerns, including low mood, anxiety, friendship concerns, low self-esteem and body image concerns. They also have a textline, providing free 24/7 support for young people concerned about their mental health.
www.youngminds.org.uk or text YM to 85258

NHS Every Mind Matters

www.nhs.uk/every-mind-matters/mental-wellbeing-tips/youth-mental-health

Mind Charity

www.mind.org.uk/for-young-people/how-to-get-help-and-support/useful-contacts